Listening Advantage

2

Tom Kenny
Tamami Wada

THOMSON

HEINLE™

Australia · Canada · Mexico · Singapore · Spain · United Kingdom · United States

D1313695

THOMSON
HEINLE

Listening Advantage, Student Book 2
Kenny / Wada

Editorial Director: Joe Dougherty
VP, Director of Content Development: Anita Raducanu
Director of Product Marketing: Amy Mabley
Director of Global Field Marketing: Ian Martin
Editorial Manager: Sean Bermingham
Development Editor: Derek Mackrell
Content Project Manager: Tan Jin Hock

Sr. Print Buyer: Mary Beth Hennebury
Compositor: CHROME Media Pte. Ltd.
Illustrator: Edwin Ng
Cover/Text Designer: CHROME Media Pte. Ltd./C. M. Hanzie
Printer: Transcontinental
Cover Images: CHROME Media Pte. Ltd./Photodisc, Inc.

For more information contact Heinle, 25 Thomson Place, Boston, Massachusetts 02210 USA. You can visit our web site at elt.heinle.com

For permission to use material from this text or product, submit a request online at http://www.thomsonrights.com Any additional questions about permissions can be submitted by e-mail to thomsonrights@thomson.com

Student Book ISBN-13: 978-1-4240-0203-0
Student Book ISBN-10: 1-4240-0203-6
Book + Audio CD ISBN-13: 978-1-4240-0194-1
Book + Audio CD ISBN-10: 1-4240-0194-3

Photo Credits
Photos.com: pages 7 (top right), 8, 12, 16 (all except bottom right), 17 (bottom row far right), 18 (all except second row right), 21 (center left), 38 (center right), 43 (center left), 46 (left and right), 50, 54 (second row left and right), 59 (second row center right and right); Index Open: pages 7 (top left and second row right), 51 (left and center left); iStockphoto: pages 7 (second row left and bottom three), 13, 16 (bottom right), 17 (all except bottom row far right), 18 (second row right), 20, 21 (all except center left), 22, 24, 26, 28, 30, 38 (all except center right), 40, 43 (all except center left), 44, 46 (center left and center right), 51 (right and center right), 54 (all except second row left and right), 59 (all except second row center right and right), 68; Landov: page 42

The authors and publisher would like to thank the following reviewers for their help during the development of this series:
Mike Bryan, Nihon University Junior/Senior High School; **David Buchanan,** St. Dominic High School; **Hsin-Hwa Chen,** Yuan Ze University; **Wong Fook Fei,** Universiti Kebangsaan; **Ding Guocheng,** Shanghai Jincai Middle School; **Caroline C. Hwang,** National Taipei University of Technology; **Michelle Misook Kim,** Kyung Hee University; **Young Hee Cheri Lee,** Reading Town USA English Language Institute; **Hae Chin Moon,** Korea University; **Chieko Okada,** Toho Senior High School; **Hiromi Okamura,** Toho Senior High School; **Kate Mastruserio Reynolds,** University of Wisconsin - Eau Claire; **Yoshi Sato,** Nagoya University of Foreign Studies; **Joe Spear,** Hanbat National University; **Keiko Takahashi,** Ikeda Senior High School; **Yanan Une-aree,** Bangkok University; **Mei-ling Wu,** Mackay Medicine, Nursing and Management College; the students and teachers of Nagoya High School

Contents

Scope and Sequence

Daily Life

Unit	Lesson	Language/Strategy	Catch It!
1 Keeping Busy *Page 8*	**A** What are you good at? **B** What club will you join?	• Talking about skill level • Repeating a question	Weak forms of prepositions
2 School *Page 12*	**A** Which classes do you like? **B** What do you think about school?	• Superlative phrases • Restating	Question tones
3 Food *Page 16*	**A** What's your favorite dish? **B** What should we eat?	• Giving reasons • Asking for and giving examples	Linking

Places and Things

Unit	Lesson	Language/Strategy	Catch It!
4 My Phone *Page 20*	**A** I use my phone for everything! **B** Which one should we get?	• Comparatives and superlatives • Reactions *(not) so* + (adj.)	Word stress
5 Music *Page 24*	**A** What do you listen to? **B** Music cheers me up.	• Giving a reason for doing something • Agreeing	Pronouncing *s*
6 Video Games *Page 28*	**A** What do you play? **B** That's a great score!	• *Try* + . . . *-ing* • Showing a strong reaction	Syllable stress

People I Know

Unit	Lesson	Language/Strategy	Catch It!
7 Meeting People *Page 38*	A Have you ever felt shy? B The weather is a safe topic.	• Asking about experience • Raising a topic	Question words
8 Heroes *Page 42*	A What kind of person do you admire? B What makes a hero?	• Relative clauses • Getting time to think	Syllables
9 Teachers *Page 46*	A He makes me interested in it. B He's such a supportive teacher.	• Saying how something makes you feel • Asking for clarification	Consonant sounds

Hopes and Dreams

Unit	Lesson	Language/Strategy	Catch It!
10 Money *Page 50*	A It's good for me to save money. B If I had a million dollars . . .	• Explaining how you feel • Reactions	Tag questions
11 Advertising *Page 54*	A I saw your ad on TV. B I guess ads entertain us.	• Requesting • Giving opinions	Using intonation to agree or disagree
12 Happiness *Page 58*	A You look so happy! B What is happiness?	• Describing people • Starting a response	The word "Well . . ."

Introduction

Listening in a foreign language is sometimes very difficult. People talk very fast and they use a lot of words and difficult language. *Listening Advantage* will help you!

Real situations and interesting topics

Listening Advantage uses situations from real life:

People in *Listening Advantage* talk about interesting things:

Useful language and pronunciation practice

Language Focus will teach you useful language from real life.

Catch It! will help you understand the way that English speakers talk.

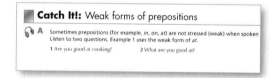

Important strategies

Conversation Strategy sections show you how to listen more actively.

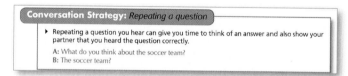

Practice your strategies in the *Talk It Over* and *Try It Out!* sections.

Test taking skills

The *Self-Study* section and *Practice Tests* give lots of listening test practice.

To become a good listener, listen as much as you can—in class and outside class. We hope you enjoy using *Listening Advantage*! Good luck!

Tom and Tamami

Useful Expressions

Could you repeat that, please?

Sorry, I don't understand.

What does this mean?

What's your answer for question 1?

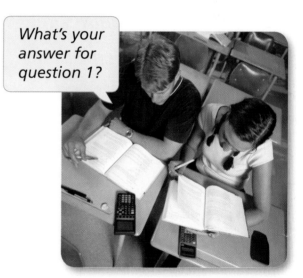

Could you turn up the volume, please?

More slowly, please.

How do you spell that?

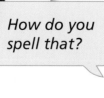

Keeping Busy

Lesson A — *What are you good at?*

Warm-up

A Here is a list of activities. Listen and fill in the blanks.

1 _____ing sports
2 _____ing sports
3 _____ing songs
4 playing _____
5 playing _____ _____
6 _____ing e-mails
7 _____ing pictures
8 _____ing _____ music

B Listen again and check your answers. Practice saying each to a partner.

Listening

A Four speakers are talking about what they like to do. Listen and number the pictures 1–4.

  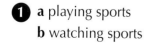  

1   **a** playing sports
     b watching sports

2   **a** looking at pictures
     b drawing pictures

3   **a** singing slow songs
     b singing fast songs

4   **a** listening to musi
     b playing music

B Listen again. Which activity does each speaker like more? Circle **a** or **b**.

Further Listening

 A Listen to four speakers talking about activities. Circle the correct activity.

① a   b   **②** a   b

③ a   b   **④** a   b

 B Listen again. What else do they say about their activity? Circle **a** or **b**.

1 **a** plays on Sunday   **b** plays on sunny days
2 **a** plays at home   **b** plays on stage
3 **a** makes cookies   **b** makes cakes
4 **a** played for six days   **b** played for three days

Language Focus: *Talking about skill level*

▸ Use this expression to talk about your skill level:
   *I'm **good** at . . .   great / good / OK / not so good / terrible*
   I'm great at playing soccer.   I'm not so good at basketball.

 C Listen again. How good at the activity is each person? Check (✔) the phrases you hear.

	1	2	3	4
good at				
OK at				
not so good at				
terrible at				

Talk It Over

Work in a group. Introduce yourself and say something you're good at and something you're not so good at.

My name is Min. I'm from Seoul.

I'm good at playing video games.

I'm not so good at cooking.

Before You Listen

A   Look at the club names. Circle the ones you think are interesting. Write the names of any other clubs you can think of.

art club	tennis club
singing club	baseball club
drama club	broadcasting club
swimming club	gymnastics club
music club	book club
_____ club	_____ club
_____ club	_____ club

B   Put a check (✔) next to the clubs that you think are the most popular for high school students. Compare your answers with a partner.

Extended Listening

A   Some friends are talking about clubs. What clubs are they thinking about joining? Listen and circle **a** or **b**.

1

2

3

4

B Listen again. Do *both* friends decide to join? Circle **yes, no,** or **undecided.**

1 **a** yes   **b** no   **c** undecided   3 **a** yes   **b** no   **c** undecided

2 **a** yes   **b** no   **c** undecided   4 **a** yes   **b** no   **c** undecided

Conversation Strategy: *Repeating a question*

▸ Repeating a question you hear can give you time to think of an answer and also show your partner that you heard the question correctly.

  A: What do you think about the soccer team?
  B: The soccer team?

C Listen again. Number the repeated questions 1–4 in the order you hear them.

What am I interested in? ____   Get some information? ____

Stay with basketball? ____   A lot of meetings? ____

Catch It!: Weak forms of prepositions

A Sometimes prepositions (for example, *in, on, at*) are not stressed (weak) when spoken quickly. Listen to two questions. Example 1 uses the weak form of *at.*

1 Are you good at cooking?   **2** What are you good at?

B Listen to the sentences. What preposition does the speaker use? Complete the sentences.

1 We can learn how _____ act.

2 What do you think _____ the baseball club?

3 We can have a lot _____ fun.

4 Do you want _____ join the art club?

5 I'll meet you _____ the park.

6 Can you think _____ anything else?

7 Do you have _____ study tonight?

Try It Out!

Write the names of three clubs. Think of a good point for each. Then ask your partner if he or she wants to join. Remember to repeat the question.

A: Do you want to join the drama club?
B: The drama club?
A: Yeah. We can learn how to act.

A: What do you think of the baseball club?
B: The baseball club?
A: Yeah. We can get a lot of exercise.

A: Do you want to join the art club?
B: The art club?
A: Yeah. We can have a lot of fun.

Club	Good Points
1	We can learn how to _____.
2	We have only _____ meetings a week.
3	We can _____.

School

Lesson A   *Which classes do you like?*

Warm-up

 A Here is a list of school subjects and classes.
Match the subjects to the classes.
Listen and check your answers.

Subject	Classes
_____ art	**a** P.E., nutrition
_____ music	**b** business, finance
_____ history	**c** algebra, calculus
_____ science	**d** drawing, painting
_____ language	**e** biology, chemistry
_____ math	**f** novels, poetry
_____ social studies	**g** geography, sociology
_____ economics	**h** journalism, grammar
_____ health	**i** Asian, European
_____ literature	**j** voice, instruments
_____ writing	**k** French, German

B Circle the subjects you like. Compare your answers with a partner.

Listening

A Four students are talking about the subjects they like. Listen and number
the illustrations 1–4.

❶ a drawing faces   **❷ a** adding numbers   **❸ a** memorizing   **❹ a** playing the piano
    b drawing buildings   **b** solving problems   **b** listening   **b** singing

 B Listen again. What are they good at? Circle **a** or **b**.

Further Listening

 A Four speakers are talking about what subjects they enjoy. Listen and number the pictures 1–4.

 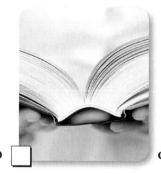  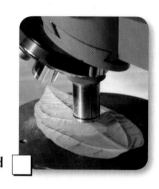

a ☐   b ☐   c ☐   d ☐

 B Listen again. Why do they like these subjects? Circle **a** or **b**.

1 **a** It helps her to know about the world.   **b** It helps her relax.

2 **a** He thinks stories are cool.   **b** He thinks people, places, and dates are cool.

3 **a** He wants to play sports.   **b** He wants to be a doctor.

4 **a** She wants to study computers.   **b** She wants to teach computers.

Language Focus: *Superlative phrases*

▸ Use this phrase to show when something is the best or worst:
the most important (difficult / fun / interesting / challenging / boring . . .)
History is **the most interesting** *subject.*

 C Listen again. Match the subjects to the phrase.

1 the most fun   **a** algebra

2 the most interesting   **b** fiction

3 the most difficult   **c** biology

4 the most important   **d** American history

Talk It Over

Work with two partners. Take turns talking about the subjects you study.

Algebra is the most fun.

Really?

Yeah. How about you?

Before You Listen

 A Look at the adjectives that describe school. Match the illustration with the correct adjective. One adjective is not used. Listen and check.

> fun   terrible   stressful   interesting   boring

1 _____   2 _____   3 _____   4 _____

B How do you usually feel at school? Write a check (✔) next to the illustrations that show your moods.

Extended Listening

A Three students are competing for the Best New Student award. Listen and match the student the items in the box. One item is not used.

> **a** most fun   **b** most difficult   **c** most exciting   **d** most terrible

1 _____ Flora   **2** _____ Ruel   **3** _____ Mei

B Listen again. What answer does each student give first? Circle **a** or **b**.

Conversation Strategy: *Restating*

▶ If you don't understand what someone said, repeat what you think you heard as a question. It's a fast way to check for understanding.

A: The soccer club is the most important thing.
B: Did you say "the soccer club"?

 C Listen again and number the questions 1–3. One of them is not used.

____ Did you say "winners get a prize"?

____ Did you say "pay teachers more"?

____ Did you say "the most fun"?

____ Did you say "the most terrible thing"?

Catch It!: Question tones

 A In checking what someone said, use a stronger tone when you are surprised. Compare the two questions.

Examples: **1** Did you say his name is Paul? (checking)

   2 Did you say his name is **Paul**? (surprised)

B Listen to the questions. Is the speaker checking or surprised?

	1	2	3	4	5	6	7
Checking							
Surprised							

Try It Out!

Write down three school subjects and an adjective for each. Then discuss with a partner. Remember to restate when listening.

Example:

A: I like studying geography.

B: Did you say "geography"?

A: Yeah. I think it's interesting.

Me	
Subject	Adjective
1	
2	
3	

My partner	
Subject	Adjective
1	
2	
3	

Food

Lesson A — *What's your favorite dish?*

Warm-up

 A Look at the food words below. Are they verbs (**V**), adjectives (**A**), or nouns (**N**)? Write **V**, **A**, or **N** next to each. Listen and check your answers.

lean	put in	chicken	chopped
beef	soy sauce	tomato	onion
potato	ground	mix	sauce
bake	cheese	carrot	pasta
cucumber	mayonnaise	lamb	shredded

B Practice saying each food word with a partner. Make a list of other food words.

Listening

A Four speakers are talking about their favorite dishes. Listen and number the pictures 1–4.

a

b

c

d

B Listen again. What extra information do they give about the dishes? Number them 1–4. One of them is not used.

____ It's easy to make.   ____ It's perfect for a picnic.

____ My mother's is the best.   ____ You never get it in a restaurant.

____ You put in expensive vegetables.

Further Listening

A Listen to the conversations about meals. Which meal are they going to have?
Number the conversations 1–4. One meal is not used.

Breakfast ___   Lunch ___   Dinner ___   Dessert ___   Snack ___

B Listen again. What food do they decide to eat? Circle **a** or **b**.

1 a b

3 a b

2 a b

4 a b

Language Focus: *Giving reasons*

▸ You can add a reason to a statement using this structure:
  I like X because + **reason**.
  I like sushi because it's light and fast to eat.

C Listen again. Number the reasons 1–4. One is not used.

____ . . . because it's healthy.   ____ . . . because it's cheap and light.

____ . . . because I'm on a diet.   ____ . . . because it's rich and delicious.

____ . . . because I don't eat them so often.

Talk It Over

Work with two partners. Talk about the
foods you like and why.

*I like to eat only vegetables because
they are tasty and healthy.*

*Really? I want to eat cheesecake
because it's fun and delicious to eat.*

Before You Listen

 A   Match the adjectives with the same meaning. One is not used. Listen and check.

1 hot	**a** quick
2 delicious	**b** cheap
3 filling	**c** juicy
4 fast	**d** tasty
5 inexpensive	**e** spicy
	f heavy

B   Practice saying each word pair with a partner.

Extended Listening

 A   It's Saturday afternoon at the mall and some friends are talking about food. Number the foods 1–5.

a

b

c

d

e

B   Listen again. Why do they want to eat the food? Match each reason to one of the foods above. Write **a–e** in the space.

1 really hot _____   **2** fast and light _____   **3** healthy and tasty _____

4 really filling _____   **5** cheap and quick _____

Conversation Strategy: *Asking for and giving examples*

▸ To make someone be more specific, use these phrases:
Like what? For example?

▸ If you hear these phrases, you can start your answer with the same phrase:
Like _____.   For example, _____.

A: You should buy something cheap.
B: Like what?
A: Like a small sandwich.

 C   Listen again. Match the adjective to the example.

1	heavy	**a**	Like chicken.
2	juicy	**b**	Like sushi.
3	spicy	**c**	Like curry.
4	simple	**d**	Like hamburgers.
5	healthy	**e**	Like fruit.

Catch It!: Linking

 A   Vowel sounds and consonant sounds are often linked together. Listen to the example below.

I'd like to eat an apple.

B   Listen to each sentence and draw a line to connect the sounds that are linked.

1 Did you just eat an orange?

2 Can you turn off the oven?

3 That's all you're going to eat?

4 You'd better drink all your juice.

5 Which bus are you taking to the restaurant?

6 What's on your shopping list?

7 I'll think about what I want for lunch.

Try It Out!

Write three adjectives to describe food. Your partner will ask for a specific example for each.

Example:

A: I want to eat something simple.

B: Like what?

A: Like tacos!

Food adjective	Example
1	Like
2	Like
3	Like

My Phone

4

Lesson A — *I use my phone for everything!*

Warm-up

A Here are some features of cell phones. Check (✔) the features that your cell phone has.

memory	____	text messaging	____
display	____	speakerphone	____
camera flash	____	flashlight	____
music player	____	Internet service	____
headset	____	battery	____

B Which cell phone features are most useful to you? Circle them. Compare with a partner.

Listening

 A Four speakers are talking about the cell phones they need. Listen and number the speakers 1–

a ☐

b ☐

c ☐

 B Listen again. What else do they say about their phone? Circle **a** or **b**.

1 **a** really need it   **b** don't really need it
2 **a** use it a lot   **b** don't use it so much
3 **a** old   **b** new
4 **a** cheap   **b** expensive

d ☐

Further Listening

 A Listen to four conversations about buying a new phone. Which phones are they talking about? Number the phones 1–4.

a ☐

b ☐

c ☐

d ☐

 B Listen again. Are these statements True (**T**) or False (**F**)?

1 She likes her old phone more than her new one.	T / F
2 He can watch TV on his phone.	T / F
3 He needs a phone with a lot of memory.	T / F
4 The phone can send e-mail.	T / F

Language Focus: *Comparatives and superlatives*

▶ **Use these words to compare things:**

good   better   best

bad   worse   worst

X is good. X is better than Y. Z is the best.

C Listen again. Number the sentences 1–4.

_____ This is the worst phone I've ever used.   _____ The best was the most expensive.

_____ This one's much better.   _____ Cheap phones are even worse.

Talk It Over

Compare the four cell phones above with a partner.

What do you think about the red phone?

It has no camera, but it has the best color!

Which one should we get?

Before You Listen

 A Match the adjectives to the mobile phone features. Some adjectives may match more than one feature. Listen and check.

round	heavy	small	cheap	big	thick
clear	display sound weight shape size price	reasonable
sharp	light	square	tiny	expensive

B Circle the words that describe your perfect phone. Tell your partner.

Extended Listening

A Miyuki and her children are shopping for new phones. Match the phones in the box to the person who wants it. One phone is not used.

> **a** VersaComm   **b** FlexFone   **c** Ultra Air   **d** MegaTel

Miyuki

Akiho

Shunji

B Listen again. What features does each phone have? Write **a–d** next to each feature.

TV ___   Internet ___   camera ___   UFO button ___

e-mail ___   video games ___   plays music ___   video camera ___

▸ Use these phrases to show your reaction to something:

so _____   *not so* _____

A: Did you see this one?   **A:** How's your new phone?
B: Yeah, it's *so light*!   **B:** It's *not so easy* to use.

 C   Listen again. How do they react to the phones? Match the adjectives the speakers use to react to each phone. Each phone matches more than one adjective.

FlexFone _____   Ultra Air _____   MegaTel _____   VersaComm _____

a so light   **c** so thin   **e** so cheap   **g** so sharp
b so big   **d** not so small   **f** so clear   **h** so heavy

Catch It!: Word stress

 A   Important words get the most stress in a sentence. Listen to the stressed words in the sample sentence.

It has E-MAIL and the INTERNET.

 B   Listen and underline the words that are stressed the most. Why do you think the speaker stressed those words? Discuss with a partner.

1 The FlexFone is so cheap.   **5** I use my phone all the time.

2 Your phone is bigger than mine.   **6** Did you see the new X-phone?

3 That phone is too heavy.   **7** He forgot his phone again.

4 That display isn't sharp enough.

Try It Out!

Look again at the phones pictured on page 21. Take turns describing the features and reacting.

Examples:

A: Did you see the display on phone b?

B: Yeah, it's so big!

Music

Lesson A *What do you listen to?*

Warm-up

A Here is a list of kinds of music.
Check (✔) the kinds you like.

pop	rap
jazz	hip-hop
classical	gospel
electronica	rock
Latin American	reggae
R & B (Rhythm & Blues)	

B Compare your list with a partner's.
How many artists can you name
for each kind of music?

Listening

A Four speakers are talking about how they make music. Listen and number the pictures 1–4.

a

b

c

d

B Listen again. What genre of music do they like? Circle **a** or **b**.

1 **a** country   **b** rock
2 **a** jazz   **b** classical
3 **a** R&B   **b** hip-hop
4 **a** pop   **b** classical

Further Listening

 A   Four people are talking about music. Listen and number the CDs 1–4.

a ☐

b ☐

c ☐

d ☐

 B   Listen again. How does the music change their mood? Number the ways 1–4. One is not used.

a _____ "it relaxes me."   **d** _____ "it calms me down."

b _____ "it makes me happy."   **e** _____ "it cheers me up."

c _____ "it gives me energy."

Language Focus: *Giving a reason for doing something*

▸ Give a personal reason for doing something by using "When . . ."

When <u>I feel lonely</u> + <u>I listen to pop music.</u>
      reason   action

 C   Listen again. When does each speaker listen to music? Number the reasons 1–4. One is not used.

a _____ "When I feel romantic . . ."   **d** _____ "When I feel sad . . ."

b _____ "When I feel emotional . . ."   **e** _____ "When I feel lazy . . ."

c _____ "When I feel nervous . . ."

Talk It Over

Work with a partner. What kind of music do you like?

> *What kind of music do you listen to?*

> *I like pop music. When I feel sad, I listen to pop music. It cheers me up. How about you?*

Music cheers me up.

Before You Listen

 A Look at these popular places and times for listening to music. Guess the missing words. Listen and check your answers.

Time	Place
_____ the morning	_____ home
_____ school	_____ my bike
_____ the evening	_____ the car
late _____ night	_____ the bus/train
_____ the weekend	_____ my room
_____ holiday	_____ my friend's house

B Where and when do *you* listen to music? Draw lines to match the times and places. Compare your answers with a partner's.

Extended Listening

 A A radio program is interviewing a popular singer. Three people call in to ask questions. Where does each caller listen to music? Number the photos 1–3. One is not used.

a ☐ b ☐ c ☐ d ☐

 B Listen again. Match the questions below to the correct person.

1 Who buys and downloads online?   **a** Lori Kool

2 Who has a big CD collection?   **b** Caller 1

3 Who borrows from friends?   **c** Caller 2

     d Caller 3

Conversation Strategy: *Agreeing*

▸ Use these phrases to agree with someone.

Positive:	*Me too.*	*So do I.*
Negative:	*Me neither.*	*Neither do I.*

Example 1: **A:** I have Lori Kool's new CD.
   B: So do I. It's great!

Example 2: **A:** I don't buy a lot of CDs.
   B: Me neither.

 C Listen again. Which phrases do they use to show they agree? Match the phrase with the sentence they agree with. One is used twice.

1 _____ I've got a nice new stereo.

2 _____ I sing along with old jazz songs.

3 _____ I don't have a lot of money!

4 _____ I buy online and download songs.

5 _____ I don't have room at home for a bunch of CDs.

a Neither do I.

b Me too.

c Me neither.

d So do I.

Catch It!: Pronouncing *s*

 A For verbs in third-person singular, such as *talks*, *gives*, or *fixes*, the *s* can be pronounced in three different ways. Listen to the *s* in the examples.

/s/ talks   /z/ gives   /ɪz/ fixes

B Listen to how each verb is pronounced and check the box.

	1	2	3	4	5	6	7
/s/							
/z/							
/ɪz/							

Try It Out!

Ask two partners about music. Remember to say when you agree with your partner.

Example:

A: What kind of music do you like?

B: I like pop music.

A: Me too. How do you get your music?

B: I borrow CDs from my friends.

	What	How	Where	When
Partner 1				
Partner 2				

Video Games

Lesson A — *What do you play?*

Warm-up

A Here are six kinds of video games. Match each one to an illustration. Listen and check.

sports	puzzle
racing	action-adventure
simulation	role-playing

a _____

b _____

c _____

d _____

B Circle your favorite kinds of games. Write an X next to the games you've never played. Discuss with a partner.

e _____

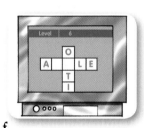

f _____

Listening

A Four speakers are talking about playing video games. Are they experienced (e) or inexperienced (i) players? Write **i** or **e**.

1 _____   2 _____   3 _____   4 _____

a ☐

b ☐

c ☐

B Listen again. Where do they play video games? Number the pictures 1–4.

d ☐

Further Listening

 A Some friends are talking about playing video games. Which game are they playing?
Listen and circle **a** or **b**.

1

2

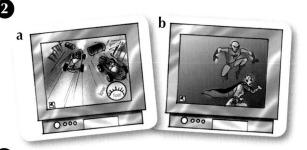

3

4

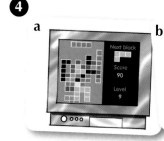 

 B Listen again. Why do they like their games? Circle a or b.

1 **a** fun to win   **b** easy to play   3 **a** takes a long time   **b** cute story
2 **a** interesting story   **b** cool effects   4 **a** have to move fast   **b** difficult to play

Language Focus: *Try + . . . -ing*

▸ I'd like to try (verb)+ing.
I'd like to try flying.

 C Listen again. Number the reasons 1–4.

_____ I'd like to try dancing.   _____ I'd like to try shooting.
_____ I'd like to try fighting.   _____ I'd like to try driving.

Talk It Over

Work with a partner. Take turns talking about three games pictured on the previous page.

> I'd like to try a flying game.

> I'd like to try a role-playing game.

> Why?

> I want to be a pilot.

> I like fantasy stories.

> Why?

Lesson B   *That's a great score!*

Before You Listen

A Different video games have different goals. Write the words in the box next to the verbs below to make goals. Listen and check.

> the race   the princess   a high score   the other player
> the mystery   a thousand points   the game   flying

get _____

win _____

solve _____

save _____

try _____

score _____

beat _____

B Work with a partner. Add other goals to the list above. Use the phrases above to talk about games you have played.

Extended Listening

A Three friends are at a video arcade talking about their favorite games. What's the goal of each game? Number the goals 1–3 in the order you hear. One is not used.

_____ find the princess   _____ solve the mystery   _____ get a high score   _____ save the world

B Listen again. What other information do they give about each game? Are these statements True (**T**) or False (**F**)?

Pac Person

1 He got one thousand points.   T / F

2 He played the game for two weeks.   T / F

First Fantasy

1 She likes the characters.   T / F

2 Her sister isn't good at the game.   T / F

Super Scario

1 He finished it quickly.   T / F

2 The game is very popular.   T / F

Conversation Strategy: *Showing a strong reaction*

▸ Use these phrases to show a strong reaction.

I don't believe it!   Are you joking?   Are you serious?   You're joking!   Seriously?

Example: **A:** I cleared the tenth level!
                B: Are you serious?

 C   What phrases do they use to react? Number the phrases 1–3. One phrase is not used.

_____ Seriously?   _____ You're joking.

_____ Are you joking?   _____ I don't believe you.

Catch It!: Syllable stress

 A   Learning syllable stress is an important part of sounding natural in English.
Listen to the example.

unbeLIEVable

B   Which syllable is stressed? Underline the stressed syllable in the words in bold.
Listen and check.

1 Are you **kidding**?   **4** I don't **believe** it!   **7** That's so **fantastic**!

2 That's **impossible**!   **5** That's **amazing**!   **8** Oh, that's **wonderful**!

3 Are you **serious**?   **6** You're **joking**!   **9** You're **terrific**!

Try It Out!

Look at the kinds of games listed in the chart. Make up a game name, a goal, and how long it took to finish each. Tell a partner.

Example:

A: I finished a sports game called Soccer Cup.   **B:** How long did it take?
B: What was the goal?   **A:** Only three days
A: To win the game.   **B:** You're joking!

Partner	Name	Goal	How long did it take?
role playing	First Fantasy	save the world	one month
sports	Soccer Cup	win the game	three days
action-adventure			
racing			
puzzle			

Practice Test

Part 1

Listen. Choose the best answer.

1 Which sport is he probably good at?

a

b

c

d

2 How many years has he been taking piano lessons?

    a 4   **b** 8   **c** 11   **d** 12

3 What club is she going to join?

    a the singing club   **b** the music club   **c** the drama club   **d** She doesn't say.

4 What is his most challenging subject?

    a history   **b** English   **c** math   **d** science

5 What is her favorite juicy food?

a

b

c

d

6 What kind of music is he listening to?

    a country   **b** jazz   **c** rock   **d** classical

Part 2

Listen. Choose the best reply.

7 **a** I wanna try.   **b** Would you like to try it?

   c Let's try it.   **d** Shall we try it?

8 **a** Does she like it?   **b** How is it?

   c Like what?   **d** Yeah, it's so cheap!

9 **a** No, I'm not hungry.   **b** Did you say "diet"?

   c The drinks are so expensive. **d** What do you think of the menu?

10 **a** It's so bright!   **b** Me, neither.

    c For example?   **d** I like it because it's expensive.

11 **a** I'd like to try flying.   **b** Do you play on your bicycle?

    c Are you kidding?   **d** Jazz is better than electronica.

12 **a** Me, too.   **b** I can't.

    c Neither do I. **d** So do I.

13 **a** It bores me.   **b** It cheers me up.

    c It gives me energy. **d** It makes me happy.

Part 3

A   Listen. Choose the best answer.

14 Which cell phone feature is NOT free?

    a Internet service   **b** text messaging

    c headset   **d** sharp display

15 Which subject is the girl good at?

    a calculus   **b** chemistry

    c math   **d** Don't know.

16 What did she lose?

    a   **b**   **c**   **d**

B   Listen. Choose the best answer (a–f) for questions 17–19.

School Survey

The most fun	The most interesting	The most difficult	The most challenging	The most boring
17	18		19	

    a algebra   **d** chemistry

    b French   **e** economics

    c P. E.   **f** art

Part 4

A Listen. Choose the best answer.

20 Who is his hero?

   a SuperSam   **b** his cousin   **c** his best friend   **d** his brother

21 What feature does the ZEN-Q cell phone NOT have?

   a camera flash   **b** speaker phone   **c** large display   **d** solar battery

22 What genre of music does she listen to in the car?

   a R&B   **b** rock   **c** classical   **d** hip-hop

B Listen. Choose the best answer.

23 Which food is the most popular?

   a Japanese   **b** Korean   **c** Italian   **d** Thai

24 What kind of Japanese food does he think is NOT healthy?

   a tempura   **b** sushi   **c** curry   **d** tonkatsu

25 What is his favorite food?

   a Chinese   **b** Korean   **c** Italian   **d** French

Practice Test 1 Answer Sheet

Part 1

1 ⓐ ⓑ ⓒ ⓓ   4 ⓐ ⓑ ⓒ ⓓ
2 ⓐ ⓑ ⓒ ⓓ   5 ⓐ ⓑ ⓒ ⓓ
3 ⓐ ⓑ ⓒ ⓓ   6 ⓐ ⓑ ⓒ ⓓ

Part 2

7 ⓐ ⓑ ⓒ ⓓ   11 ⓐ ⓑ ⓒ ⓓ
8 ⓐ ⓑ ⓒ ⓓ   12 ⓐ ⓑ ⓒ ⓓ
9 ⓐ ⓑ ⓒ ⓓ   13 ⓐ ⓑ ⓒ ⓓ
10 ⓐ ⓑ ⓒ ⓓ

Part 3

14 ⓐ ⓑ ⓒ ⓓ   17 ⓐ ⓑ ⓒ ⓓ ⓔ ⓕ
15 ⓐ ⓑ ⓒ ⓓ   18 ⓐ ⓑ ⓒ ⓓ ⓔ ⓕ
16 ⓐ ⓑ ⓒ ⓓ   19 ⓐ ⓑ ⓒ ⓓ ⓔ ⓕ

Part 4

A   **B**

20 ⓐ ⓑ ⓒ ⓓ   23 ⓐ ⓑ ⓒ ⓓ
21 ⓐ ⓑ ⓒ ⓓ   24 ⓐ ⓑ ⓒ ⓓ
22 ⓐ ⓑ ⓒ ⓓ   25 ⓐ ⓑ ⓒ ⓓ

Meeting People

Lesson A   *Have you ever felt shy?*

Warm-up

A Read the statements about meeting new people. Are these stories true for you?
Circle Yes (**Y**) or No (**N**).

1	I like meeting new people.	Y / N
2	I'm quite shy.	Y / N
3	I'd like to have more friends.	Y / N
4	I'm usually afraid to talk to strangers.	Y / N
5	I'll talk to strangers if they talk to me first.	Y / N
6	I can make friends quickly.	Y / N

B Compare your answers with a partner's. How many did you answer the same?

Listening

 A Four speakers are talking about where they meet new people. Listen and number the places 1–4

a ☐   b ☐   c ☐   d ☐

 B Listen again. Why do they recommend these places? Number the reasons 1–4.

a ___ It's easy to start conversations.   **c** ___ You make friends with co-workers.

b ___ You meet people who share your interests.   **d** ___ It's good to know your neighbors.

Further Listening

A A reporter is asking four students about meeting new people.
Are the students shy or not shy? Circle **a** or **b**.

1 **a** shy   **b** not shy
2 **a** shy   **b** not shy
3 **a** shy   **b** not shy
4 **a** shy   **b** not shy

B Listen again. Are these statements
True (**T**) or False (**F**)?

1 She worries about saying something wrong. _____
2 He sometimes get nervous. _____
3 He smiles at people he doesn't know. _____
4 She sometimes talks to strangers. _____

Language Focus: *Asking about experience*

▸ **Use this question to ask about experience.**
   Have you ever + past participle form of verb (met, spoken, done)?
   Have you ever *met someone famous?*
   Have you ever *spoken to a celebrity?*

C Listen again. Write the missing past participles.

1 Have you ever _____ a conversation?
2 Have you ever _____ shy?
3 Have you ever _____ someone you don't know?
4 Have you ever _____ a stranger?

Talk It Over

Work with a partner. Take turns asking questions about your experience.

> Have you ever
> eaten Indian food?

> Yes, I have. I ate Indian
> food last week. /
> No, I haven't.

Lesson B *The weather is a safe topic.*

Before You Listen

A Look at the topics. Circle the ones you like to talk about. Write two other topics you like to talk about.

> weather   sports   TV   politics   economy
> movies   music   crime   school
> _____   _____

B Which topics do you think most high school students like to talk about? Check (✔) them. Compare answers with a partner.

Extended Listening

A A professor is giving advice about how to talk to people you've just met. Match the points to the examples.

1 _____ safe, good topic
2 _____ best topic
3 _____ topic to avoid
4 _____ after the opening topic

   a politics
   b sports, entertainment
   c the weather
   d the other person

B Listen again. According to Dr. Salley, are these statements True (**T**) or False (**F**)?

1 Severe weather is a safe topic to talk about.   T / F
2 Compliments make people talk about themselves.   T / F
3 Age is a personal topic.   T / F
4 It's OK to talk about yourself a lot.   T / F

Conversation Strategy: *Raising a topic*

▸ To introduce a new topic, you can use these questions:

What do you think about _____?   Did you _____?

Examples: What do you think about **that video game**?

Did you **see that new TV show last night**?

C Listen again. What topics are raised with these phrases? Number the topics 1–4 in the order you hear them.

_____ baseball game   _____ war

_____ hair   _____ weather

Catch It!: Question words

A Question words (who, when, where, what, why) can sound similar in natural speech. Listen to the examples.

When can I call you?   Where can I meet you?

B Listen to the sentences. Circle the question word the speaker uses.

1 Where / Why   5 What / When
2 When / Where   6 Where / When
3 What / Who   7 Why / Where
4 What / Who

Try It Out!

Imagine you just met someone and you want to start up a conversation. Write three or four good topics for conversation openers in the box below. Then work with a partner to make some opening statements or questions. Practice starting up a conversation.

Example:

A: Did you see that game last night?

B: Yes! It was great.

Topic	Opener
Baseball game	Did you see that game last night?

Heroes

Lesson A | *What kind of person do you admire?*

Warm-up

 A Look at the words in the box. Which are fields of work (**F**) and which are personality descriptions (**P**)? Listen and check.

> science   confident   athletics   music
> successful   fashionable   creative   business
> art   talented   education   organized

B Which of the fields in the box are you most interested in? Rank them (1 = most interested). Compare with a partner.

Listening

 A Four people are talking about heroes in different fields. Number the fields 1–4.

a ☐   b ☐   c ☐   d ☐

 B Listen again. What else do they say about these heroes?

1 She's . . .
   a lucky.   **b** strong and skillful.
2 She's fighting . . .
   a for her country.   **b** against war.

3 He's . . .
   a good-looking.   **b** multi-talented.
4 He's a . . .
   a typical hero.   **b** genius.

Further Listening

A Some friends are talking about qualities they admire. Which people are they describing? Listen and number the people 1–4.

a ☐

b ☐

c ☐

d ☐

B Listen again. Is each statement below True (**T**) or False (**F**)?

1 Fashionable people look confident.   T / F
2 Pop singers are heroes.   T / F
3 Intelligent people speak well.   T / F
4 Wealth is more important than success.   T / F

Language Focus: *Relative clauses*

▸ When describing people, use the phrase "people who are _____" as a subject or an object in a sentence:
*I respect people **who are** brave.*
*People **who are** brave are heroes.*

C Listen again. Number the sentences 1–4 in the order you hear them.

a _____ I respect people who are intelligent.
b _____ People who are creative get my attention.
c _____ I admire people who are fashionable.
d _____ People who are successful impress me.

Talk It Over

Think about your heroes. What qualities do they have? Tell a partner.

I admire people who are talented.

Like who?

Like Rain.

Before You Listen

A Read the various qualities of a hero. Draw a line to match each word with its definition.

1	brave	**a**	has a smart mind
2	helpful	**b**	has a powerful body
3	strong	**c**	is kind and respectful
4	intelligent	**d**	gives assistance to others
5	honest	**e**	isn't afraid of danger
6	polite	**f**	doesn't tell lies
7	talented	**g**	has natural skill

B Circle the three qualities that you think are most important for a hero to have. Compare your answers with a partner's.

Extended Listening

A George and his two children are talking about a new movie. Check (✔) the words they use to describe a hero.

a	_____	strong
b	_____	talented
c	_____	intelligent
d	_____	polite
e	_____	honest
f	_____	helpful
g	_____	creative
h	_____	brave

B Read the questions, then listen again. Circle the best answer.

1 Why do we need heroes?
  a They never tell lies.   **b** They have entertaining qualities.
  c They show us how to behave.

2 According to the father, what's the most important quality for a hero?
  a To be the best at something.   **b** To help people.   **c** To be interesting.

3 Who says politeness is an important quality?
  a the father   **b** the girl   **c** the boy

▸ Use these expressions when you need time to think after a question.
That's a(n) good / difficult / interesting / tough question.

Example: **A:** Why is the sky blue?

B: Wow, that's a difficult question . . .

C How does George get time to think? Match the questions his children ask to the expressions he uses before answering. One expression is not used.

1 Why is he a hero?

2 Why do we need heroes?

3 Is that the most important quality?

a That's an interesting question . . .

b That's a difficult question . . .

c That's a tough question . . .

d That's a good question . . .

Catch It!: Syllables

A An easy English rule to remember is that there is one syllable for each vowel sound. Listen to the examples below.

business /bɪz•nes/
creative /kri:•ei•tɪv/
confident /kɒn•fe•dənt/

B Listen. How many syllables does each word have? Write the number on the line.

1 _____   **3** _____   **5** _____   **7** _____

2 _____   **4** _____   **6** _____

Try It Out!

Write the names of two heroes and the qualities that make them heroes.
Then share them with a partner.

Example:

A: Who's your hero?

B: Ichiro.

A: Why is he your hero?

B: That's a good question.
Because he's talented.

Name	Quality
Ichiro	talented at baseball

Teachers

Lesson A   *He makes me interested in it.*

Warm-up

 A Look at these adjectives for describing a person. Draw lines to match ones with similar meanings. Not all are used. Listen and check.

strict	motivating
patient	dull
entertaining	tough
serious	fair
knowledgeable	calm
inspiring	interesting
fascinating	funny
boring	intelligent

B Which are the most important for a teacher to have? Circle three adjectives from A. Compare them with a partner's.

Listening

 A Four students are talking about their classes and teachers. Number the classes 1–4.

a

b

c

d

 B Listen again. What do they say about the teachers? Number the descriptions 1–4.

    a strict _____
    b boring _____
    c motivating _____
    d funny _____

Further Listening

A Some friends are talking about their classes. What subject does each teacher teach? Write the subject below the picture.

Mr. Hand

Mrs. Rundle

Mr. Bermingham

Ms. Gonzales

B Listen again. Which adjective describes each teacher?

1	**a** inspiring	**b** curious
2	**a** interesting	**b** tough
3	**a** entertaining	**b** knowledgeable
4	**a** intelligent	**b** patient

Language Focus: *Saying how something makes you feel*

▸ **To say how something or someone makes you feel, you can use this phrase:**
(person or thing) *makes me* + adjective phrase

She *makes me* **excited** *about science.*
Shopping *makes me* **hungry**.

C Listen again. Match to complete the sentences. One is not used.

1 "She makes me curious about . . ."   **a** learning.
2 "She makes me interested in . . ."   **b** listening to lectures.
3 "He makes me tired from . . ."   **c** taking notes.
4 "He makes me excited about . . ."   **d** science.
                                            e history.

Talk It Over

Work with a partner and talk about your teachers.

> *I like Mrs. Newman. She's so knowledgeable.*

> *Yeah, she makes me really curious about geography.*

Before You Listen

 A   Use the words from the box to fill in the blanks. Then listen and check your answers.

> dedicated   supportive   encouraging   frightening   enthusiastic

A **1** _____ teacher works with students outside of the class.

A **2** _____ teacher helps students when they don't understand, for example, by explaining things. She uses **3** _____ words, never

4 _____ words to scare students. An excited, **5** _____

teacher can make learning fun!

B   Circle the word that you think is the most important quality in a teacher. Compare your answer with a partner's.

Extended Listening

 A   Three students are discussing which teacher they will recommend for "Teacher of the Year." Match the teachers with the descriptions.

1 Mr. Ryan	**a**	really intelligent
2 Mrs. Lafferty	**b**	a little bit scary
3 Mr. Peters	**c**	a new teacher
4 Ms. Jones	**d**	totally dedicated

 B   Listen again. What other adjectives do the students use to describe each teacher? Circle **a** or **b**.

1	**a** interesting	**b**	motivating
2	**a** supportive	**b**	tough
3	**a** fair	**b**	frightening
4	**a** entertaining	**b**	serious

▶ When you don't understand why a speaker said a word, use this phrase:

What do you mean by _____?

Example: **A:** Of all our teachers, Mr. Mackrell is the most entertaining.

B: What do you mean by "entertaining"?

A: He's funny. Students are always laughing in his class.

 C Match the words from the conversations with the explanations.

1	enthusiastic	**a**	has energy
2	encouraging	**b**	works hard
3	scary	**c**	is honest
4	fair	**d**	makes me afraid
5	dedicated	**e**	gives me support

Catch It!: Consonant sounds

 A Many consonant sounds in English can be easily confused. Listen to the example. Circle the word that you hear.

hair / fair

 B Listen. Circle the word that you hear.

1 right / light	**4** pouring / boring	**7** fall / hall	**10** wine / vine
2 fan / van	**5** very / berry	**8** chin / shin	**11** copy / coffee
3 think / sink	**6** rent / lent	**9** rope / robe	**12** then / zen

Try It Out!

Use a dictionary to find two new adjectives. Define these adjectives with other words you already know. Then practice clarifying the meaning of the words with a partner.

Example:

A: This class is very useful.

B: What do you mean by "useful"?

A: I can use it in my real life.

It is helpful.

New adjective	Word with similar meaning
useful	helpful

Money

Lesson A   *It's good for me to save money.*

Warm-up

A   Read the statements about money. Circle the number that describes you:
1 = disagree strongly to 5 = agree strongly.

1	I am good at saving money.	**1 2 3 4 5**
2	I spend money quickly.	**1 2 3 4 5**
3	I want more money than I have now.	**1 2 3 4 5**
4	I get an allowance.	**1 2 3 4 5**
5	There are many things I want to buy.	**1 2 3 4 5**
6	I borrow money from friends.	**1 2 3 4 5**
7	I lend money to my friends.	**1 2 3 4 5**

B   Compare your answers with a partner's. How many are the same?

Listening

 A   Four high school students are talking about money. How does each speaker get money? Number each way in the order you hear them.

a   allowance _____

c   baby-sitting _____

b   gift money _____

d   fast-food job _____

 B   Listen again. Match each speaker's country and currency to how much that person gets.

> **a** 70,000 per year   **b** 80 per month   **c** 65 per week   **d** 3,400 per hour

1 ____

2 ____

3 ____

4 ____

Further Listening

A Four students are being asked about their money habits. Is each speaker better at making money (**M**), spending money (**Sp**), or saving money (**Sa**)?

1 _____ 2 _____ 3 _____ 4 _____

B Listen again. How are they going to use their money? Number the answers in the order you hear them.

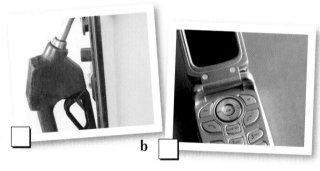

a ☐

b ☐

c ☐

d ☐

Language Focus: *Explaining how you feel*

▶ To say how something makes you feel, you can use this expression:
  It's (adjective) *for me* + infinitive.
  It's fun for me to spend money on clothes.

C Listen again. How does each person feel? Complete the sentences.

a It's _____ for me to buy something new.
b It's _____ for me to save money.
c It's _____ for me to make some money.
d It's _____ for me to borrow money from friends.

Talk It Over

Work with a partner. Take turns asking and answering questions about how you spend money.

What do you spend money on?

Clothes.

Why?

It's fun for me to buy new clothes.

Before You Listen

A Read the sentences below. If you had a million dollars, what would you do with it?
Order the sentences 1–6 (1 = first).

_____ I'd buy a big house for my family.

_____ I'd buy nice things for myself.

_____ I'd give money to help the poor.

_____ I'd start a business.

_____ I'd travel everywhere.

_____ I'd invest the money.

B Discuss your list with a partner.
Are they the same? Can you think
of any other ideas?

Extended Listening

A A TV reporter is interviewing a band. How does she describe each band member?
Match the person to the adjective. Some are not used.

1	John	**a**	the quiet one
2	Miki	**b**	the serious one
3	Derek	**c**	the fun one
		d	the romantic one
		e	the funny one

B Listen again. Are these statements True (**T**) or False (**F**)?

1 John bought a castle in New York.   T / F

2 Miki got a new car.   T / F

3 Derek invested all his money.   T / F

Conversation Strategy: *Reactions*

▸ When you want to react to something, say:

That's _____!

Positive: nice / cool / interesting / lovely / great

Negative: terrible / awful / too bad / tough

C Listen again. What does "that" refer to in these sentences?

1 _____ That's nice.   **a** a castle in France
2 _____ That's tough.   **b** becoming a millionaire
3 _____ That's lovely.   **c** playing 200 concerts a year
4 _____ That's fantastic.   **d** making money in the stock market

Catch It!: Tag questions

A Tag questions are sometimes used for confirming and sometimes for asking. Listen to the examples.

You're 16 years old, aren't you?   **confirming**
You won't go shopping today, will you?   **asking**

B Listen. Are the tag questions in these sentences asking or confirming?

1 Asking / Confirming   5 Asking / Confirming
2 Asking / Confirming   6 Asking / Confirming
3 Asking / Confirming   7 Asking / Confirming
4 Asking / Confirming

Try It Out!

Write five things you would do if you became rich. Then tell your partner.

Example:

A: If you had a million dollars, what would you do?
B: I'd buy a tropical island.
A: That's great. What else . . . ?

My To-Do List: Things I want to do when I become rich

Example: buy a tropical island

1. _____
2. _____
3. _____
4. _____
5. _____

Advertising

Lesson A   *I saw your ad on TV.*

Warm-up

 A Where can you see or hear advertisements? Write the words in the box under the correct picture. One is not used. Then listen and check.

> TV   newspaper   radio   Internet   magazine   public transportation   billboard

a _____

b _____

c _____

d _____

e _____

f _____

B Where do you most often see advertising? Circle three photos. Compare your answers with a partner's.

Listening

A Four people are talking about where they usually see advertising. Number the places 1–4 in the order you hear them. One is not used.

a _____ on TV   c _____ on the Internet   e _____ in the newspaper
b _____ on the train   d _____ billboards

B Listen again. What kind of advertisements do the speakers pay attention to? Number them in the order you hear them. One is not used.

a _____ cars   c _____ local events   e _____ bargain sales
b _____ restaurants   d _____ electronics

Further Listening

A Four people decide to go shopping after seeing store advertisements. Listen to the conversations and number the stores 1–4.

a ☐

b ☐

c ☐

d ☐

B Listen again. What do they want to buy? Circle **a** or **b**.

1 **a** desk
   b desk and a chair

2 **a** CD
   b CD with DVD

3 **a** red shoes
   b black shoes

4 **a** 32-inch display TV
   b 100-inch display TV

Language Focus: *Requesting*

▸ Use this expression to ask for something:
Could you / Can you + verb?
A: **Could you** give me a discount?
B: **Positive:** Sure. / No problem. / OK.   **Negative:** No, sorry. / I can't.

C Listen again. Complete the phrases in the order you hear them.

1 Could you _____ one with a matching chair?
2 Can you _____ when it'll be in stock?
3 Could you _____ if you have them in red?
4 Can you _____ it to my home?

Talk It Over

Work with a partner. Take turns making requests.

Could you give me a pencil?

No, sorry. I don't have one.

Can you open the window, please?

Sure.

Lesson B   *I guess ads entertain us.*

Before You Listen

A Read the statements about advertising. How strongly do you agree with each statement
(1 = disagree strongly, 5 = agree strongly)?

1 Advertising can be artistic.	**1 2 3 4 5**
2 Ads can be dangerous.	**1 2 3 4 5**
3 Entertaining ads are the most effective.	**1 2 3 4 5**
4 I'm easily pursuaded by ads.	**1 2 3 4 5**
5 Ads sometimes make me buy things I don't need.	**1 2 3 4 5**
6 TV ads are usually more effective than magazine ads.	**1 2 3 4 5**
7 Ads should be informative.	**1 2 3 4 5**

B Discuss your answers with a partner. Can you think of any other statements about
advertising that you strongly agree or disagree with?

Extended Listening

 A A professor is talking to his media class about the power of advertising.
He mentions three effects (E) and three dangers (D) of advertising. Listen and write **D**
or **E** next to each.

1 _____ Advertising makes us uncomfortable.
2 _____ Advertising entertains us.
3 _____ Advertising creates desire.
4 _____ Advertising informs us.
5 _____ Advertising persuades us.
6 _____ Advertising uses your emotions.

 B Listen again. According to the professor,
are the following statements True (**T**) or
False (**F**)?

1 Lectures are an effective form of advertising.	T / F
2 Advertising has a positive effect on the mind.	T / F
3 Advertising is most often used for products you don't really need.	T / F
4 Television ads use emotions to persuade us.	T / F

▸ Some phrases you can use to gently give your opinion are:

I guess . . . / Perhaps . . . / Maybe . . .

I guess advertising has a strong effect.

Perhaps sometimes ads can be negative.

 C Listen to how the speakers give their opinions. Match the phrases to make complete sentences. One opinion phrase is used twice.

1 I guess . . .
2 Perhaps . . .
3 Maybe . . .

    a they can be interesting.
    b that's how TV ads persuade us.
    c that's not so bad.
    d that does make them dangerous.

Catch It!: Using intonation to agree or disagree

 A You can use intonation to show whether you agree or disagree with a statement or question. Listen to the examples.

Examples: You watch TV?   Yes, I do.   (agreeing)
             You don't watch TV?   Yes, I do.   (disagreeing)

 B Listen to the conversations. Does the second speaker agree or disagree with the first speaker?

1 Agree / Disagree
2 Agree / Disagree
3 Agree / Disagree
4 Agree / Disagree

5 Agree / Disagree
6 Agree / Disagree
7 Agree / Disagree

Try It Out!

Think of three ads you remember, that you think are effective. In the table below, write the name of the product, and why you think the ad is effective. Then discuss your answers with a partner.

Example:

A: I think the TV ad for Groover Jeans works really well.

B: What do you like about it?

A: I guess, it makes me laugh, and makes me want to buy them.

Product	Why is it effective?

Happiness

Lesson A — *You look so happy!*

Warm-up

A Here are some reasons for happiness. Which ones bring you happiness? Circle three.

> family   health   money   friends   possessions
> love   career   fun   comfort   education

B Rank your top three reasons for happiness from 1–3. Compare your answers with a partner's. Can you think of any others?

Listening

A Four people are talking about what makes them happy. For each conversation, circle **a** or **b**.

❶
a   b

❷
a   b

❸
a   b

❹
a   b

B Listen again. What does each speaker say about happiness?

1 Happiness means enjoying _____.
2 Happiness is doing _____.
3 Happiness is getting _____.
4 Happiness is having a good _____.

Further Listening

A Some friends are talking about their photographs. Which photograph is being described?

❶

❷

❸

❹

 B Listen again. The speakers explain why they felt happy in their photographs. Number the reasons 1–4 in the order you hear them.

a _____ Now I can make some money!

b _____ I can do anything I want with my life.

c _____ I'd been waiting my whole life for that day.

d _____ It's the best time for me to see my family.

Language Focus: *Describing people*

▸ Use this expression to describe people:

You look [*so / very / really*] + <u>adj</u> . . .

You look so <u>handsome</u> in this picture.

 C Listen again. How is each person in the photograph described by their friend? Circle the correct word.

1 **a** excited
   b cold

2 **a** nervous
   b serious

3 **a** happy
   b tired

4 **a** thrilled
   b bored

Talk It Over

Use a picture of yourself or draw one. Listen to your partner describe how you look in the picture. Then tell your partner about that day.

You look very happy.

Yes! I enjoyed the day with my family. We went to the zoo.

Before You Listen

A Check the meaning of the words in bold. Then decide what you think. Circle **Agree** or **Disagree**.

1 It's **selfish** to want expensive things.	Agree / Disagree
2 Happiness is **connected** with kindness to other people.	Agree / Disagree
3 Everyone **deserves** happiness.	Agree / Disagree
4 Happiness **depends** on family life.	Agree / Disagree
5 Everyone can **achieve** happiness.	Agree / Disagree
6 Happiness is **influenced** by money.	Agree / Disagree
7 Happiness means you're **satisfied** with your life.	Agree / Disagree
8 Happiness is decided by **brain chemistry**.	Agree / Disagree

B Compare your opinions with a partner's. How many do you have that are the same? Which statements do you most strongly agree or disagree with?

Extended Listening

A Three students are discussing the question, "What is happiness?" Match the students to their opinion. One opinion is not used.

Consuela _____   **Pete** _____   **Kaori** _____

a Getting things you want leads to happiness.

b You get happiness by doing good for others.

c You feel happiness when other people are nice to you.

d Happiness comes from chemicals in your brain.

B Listen again. According to the speakers, are the following statements True (**T**) or False (**F**)?

1 It is possible to be poor and still be happy.	T / F
2 If you help other people, you deserve to be happy.	T / F
3 It's OK to be selfish if it makes you happy.	T / F

▶ "Well" is often used by English speakers to begin responses.
  A: What do you think?
  B: Well, maybe the reason is . . .

C Listen for the phrases that begin with "Well." Who says each one. Write Consuela (**C**), Pete (**P**), or Kaori (**K**).

a _____ Well, I know I'm not unhappy.   **c** _____ Well, that's my idea, anyway.

b _____ Well, um, I think happiness . . .   **d** _____ Well, maybe you're right.

Catch It!: The word "Well . . ."

A Listen to the intonation of "Well . . ." in these examples. "Well" can be used to soften a comment. Or to show the speaker is thinking carefully about what to say next.

To soften:
A: What does happiness mean to you?
B: Well, I guess it means being satisfied with your life.

To get time to think:
A: What does happiness mean to you?
B: Well, I guess it means being satisfied with your life.

B Listen to the sentences and decide if the speaker is softening the answer or getting time to think.

1 **a** softening **b** getting time   5 **a** softening **b** getting time
2 **a** softening **b** getting time   6 **a** softening **b** getting time
3 **a** softening **b** getting time   7 **a** softening **b** getting time
4 **a** softening **b** getting time

Try It Out!

Write three things that make you happy and explain why. Then ask your partner.

Example:

A: What makes you happy?

B: Helping people makes me happy.

A: Why?

B: Well, I guess it makes me happy
      to make other people happy!

Makes me happy	Makes my partner happy

Practice Test

Part 1

Listen. Choose the best answer.

1 When was the first time she met her boyfriend?

    a kindergarten   **b** senior high school

    c junior high school   **d** university

2 What is he probably going to talk about first with his girlfriend's parents?

a

b

c

d

3 What quality in a friend is most important to her?

    a talent   **b** honesty

    c fashion sense   **d** intelligence

4 What kind of teacher is Mr. Smith?

    a strict   **b** relaxed

    c knowledgeable   **d** All of the above.

5 How many part-time jobs does she have?

    a 1   **b** 2   **c** 3   **d** none

6 How did she spend her money at the mall?

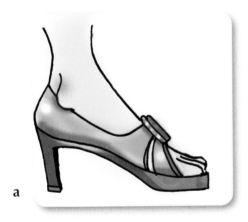

a

b

c

d

Part 2

Listen. Choose the best reply.

7   **a** No, I didn't.   **c** So do I.

     b Me, neither.   **d** Me, too.

8   **a** I don't know her.   **c** He is Indian.

     b Why do you like India?   **d** Why is he a hero?

9   **a** That's tough!   **c** Are you serious?

     b It's fun for me to go to his class.   **d** That's nice!

10 **a** That's awful.   **c** I can't afford a new one.

     b I'm good at making money.   **d** Did you say "new game"?

11 **a** Could you give me a job?   **c** Three jobs is too many!

     b You have so many CDs.   **d** I guess you work really hard.

12 **a** You look so handsome!   **c** Are you happy now?

     b Are you influenced by money? **d** I don't think about happiness.

13 **a** You don't pay attention, do you?   **c** Perhaps you should watch TV.

     b I guess you can't stand TV.   **d** I guess ads really influence us.

Part 3

A   Listen. Choose the best answer.

14   How does she make money?

a

b

c

d

15   What does she say is a good question to ask?

   a How are you?

   b What do you do?

   c Where are you from?

   d What's something you are good at?

16   What does he think is the most important quality in a relationship?

   a fun   **b** comfort   **c** honesty   **d** love

B   Listen. Choose the best answer (a–f) for questions 17–19.

Schedule for Tuesday

Supermarket	Convenience store	CD rental store	Dinny's restaurant	Park	School
17	**18**		**19**		

   a 3 p.m. to 5 p.m.

   b 5:30 p.m. to 9 p.m.

   c 5:30 p.m. to 2 a.m.

   d 10 p.m. to 2 a.m.

   e 12 p.m. to 2 a.m.

   f 2 a.m. to 3 a.m.

Part 4

A   Listen. Choose the best answer.

20   What topic did she NOT talk about with the people at the festival?

     a   weather   **b**   sports

     c   fashion   **d**   politics

21   What kind of people does she admire?

     a   people who take on new challenges   **b**   people who get rich at a young age

     c   people who have a lot of money   **d**   people who have an easy life

22   Where is the sale NOT being advertised?

     a   on the TV   **b**   on the Internet

     b   on the train   **d**   in the newspaper

B   Listen. Choose the best answer.

23   What's a tough topic to talk to her about?

     a   war   **b**   sports   **c**   movies   **d**   weather

24   Why can politics sometimes be interesting to talk about?

     a   Because war makes people uncomfortable.

     b   Because strangers love to talk about politics.

     c   Because we can learn about different ways of thinking.

     d   Because the weather can be a boring topic.

25   Why is discussing world problems useful?

     a   Because strangers can become friends.

     b   Because it could help us find a solution.

     c   Because it's OK to disagree.

     d   Because politics is too difficult

Practice Test 2 Answer Sheet

Part 1

1 ⓐ ⓑ ⓒ ⓓ   4 ⓐ ⓑ ⓒ ⓓ
2 ⓐ ⓑ ⓒ ⓓ   5 ⓐ ⓑ ⓒ ⓓ
3 ⓐ ⓑ ⓒ ⓓ   6 ⓐ ⓑ ⓒ ⓓ

Part 2

7 ⓐ ⓑ ⓒ ⓓ   11 ⓐ ⓑ ⓒ ⓓ
8 ⓐ ⓑ ⓒ ⓓ   12 ⓐ ⓑ ⓒ ⓓ
9 ⓐ ⓑ ⓒ ⓓ   13 ⓐ ⓑ ⓒ ⓓ
10 ⓐ ⓑ ⓒ ⓓ

Part 3

14 ⓐ ⓑ ⓒ ⓓ   17 ⓐ ⓑ ⓒ ⓓ ⓔ ⓕ
15 ⓐ ⓑ ⓒ ⓓ   18 ⓐ ⓑ ⓒ ⓓ ⓔ ⓕ
16 ⓐ ⓑ ⓒ ⓓ   19 ⓐ ⓑ ⓒ ⓓ ⓔ ⓕ

Part 4

A   **B**
20 ⓐ ⓑ ⓒ ⓓ   23 ⓐ ⓑ ⓒ ⓓ
21 ⓐ ⓑ ⓒ ⓓ   24 ⓐ ⓑ ⓒ ⓓ
22 ⓐ ⓑ ⓒ ⓓ   25 ⓐ ⓑ ⓒ ⓓ

Introduction to the Self-Study Units

Everyone needs more listening practice. So, after you finish each unit, go to the self-study section. Listen to the CD in the back of the book and take the 10-point quiz.

Sometimes you'll fill in the missing words. Sometimes you'll answer questions. Write your answers on the side of the page.

The CD is yours, so listen as many times as you want!

Good luck!!

 A   Listen. Choose the correct answer.

TRACK
1

Total ____

Teacher:	What sport do you like playing?
Boy:	I like playing **a** baseball ₁ **b** basketball.
Teacher:	So are you good at it?
Boy:	No, I'm **a** not so good ₂ **b** terrible at it.
Teacher:	Oh yeah? Well, what are you good at?
Boy:	Good at? Um, **a** singing ₃ **b** swimming.
Teacher:	Oh. So then what do you think about that **a** club ₄ **b** team?
Boy:	Actually, I decided to join the **a** baseball ₅ **b** basketball club this year.
Teacher:	Really? Why?
Boy:	Well, because they practice **a** in ₆ **b** at that cool, new gym.

1 ___

2 ___

3 ___

4 ___

5 ___

6 ___

 B   Listen. Choose the correct answer.

TRACK
2

7 What's she good at baking?

  a cookies   **c** bread

  b cakes   **d** pizza

7 ___

8 Which club is she NOT in now?

  a the music club   **c** the tennis club

  b the singing club   **d** the swimming club

8 ___

9 What does he want to be?

  a a director   **c** a singer

  b a drummer   **d** an actor

9 ___

10 Which club is he in?

  a the baseball club   **c** the running club

  b the tennis club   **d** the book club

10 ___

Self-Study

Total ____

1 ___

2 ___

3 ___

4 ___

5 ___

6 ___

7 ___

8 ___

9 ___

10 ___

 A Listen. Choose the correct answer.

TRACK 3

A: What would you say is your most **a** fun ₁ **b** interesting subject in school?

B: I like **a** P.E. ₂ **b** math.

A: I thought so! I always see you outside.

B: But I also really like **a** social studies ₃ **b** writing.

A: What do you think is your most challenging subject?

B: Definitely science. How about you?

A: Music is **a** hard ₄ **b** easy for me. But it's also my most interesting subject.

B: Do you play any instruments?

A: Did you say instruments?

B: That's right.

A: No, but I want to learn how to play one.

B: I guess we have very **a** different ₅ **b** exciting interests!

B Listen. Choose the best reply.

TRACK 4

6 **a** Because Monday is my most fun day at school.
b Because it's my most interesting day at school.
c Because it's my most difficult day at school.
d Because Friday is my most exciting day at school.

7 **a** That's right.
b No, I said history.
c Social studies is the most challenging.
d I don't really like history.

8 **a** Are you good at golf?
b Can I see your golf club?
c Do you like it?
d When did you quit the tennis club?

9 **a** No, it's my best subject.
b No, it's my worst subject.
c No, I love it.
d No, I like algebra.

10 **a** Biology is so easy.
b Why are you studying?
c Did you say chemistry?
d My teacher is so nice.

Self-Study

A Listen. Complete the sentences using the words in the box.

Total ____

TRACK 5

| a idea | b hamburgers | c choice | d healthy | e fried chicken | f light | g filling |

A: I'm hungry.

B: Me, too. Let's get something to eat.

A: Shall we get some sandwiches? I like them because they're **1** _____.

1 ___

B: How about something juicy? Like **2** _____.

2 ___

A: No way! Let's get something **3** _____.

3 ___

B: For example?

A: Fruit!

B: That's not **4** _____.

4 ___

A: That's true. How about sushi?

B: Yeah, then we can eat as much as we want. Sushi is a good **5** _____.

5 ___

B Listen. Choose the correct answer.

TRACK 6

6 What does the man want to do?

6 ___

  a have orange juice   **c** drink apple juice

  b eat hamburgers   **d** drink something juicy

7 What do they like about stew?

7 ___

  a It's healthy.   **c** It's tasty.

  b It's filling.   **d** All of the above.

8 What are they going to buy?

8 ___

  a potatoes   **c** onions

  b mushrooms   **d** carrots

9 Which food is chopped?

9 ___

  a cheese   **c** beef

  b lettuce   **d** tacos

10 What will he probably eat now?

10 ___

  a apple   **c** sugar

  b chocolate   **d** banana

Self-Study

Total _____

A
TRACK 7

Listen. Complete the sentences using the words in the box.

> **a** the best   **b** so   **c** sharp   **d** better   **e** big   **f** clear   **g** not so

A: Have you decided which cell phone you want?

B: I'm not sure. There are so many choices! This black one looks good. The display is so **1** _____.

A: Did you see this red one? I think it's **2** _____. And it has a large memory, which you'll find very useful.

B: But it's so **3** _____! I really want a lightweight one.

A: OK, then this green one is **4** _____.

B: But the color green is **5** _____ great. How about that blue one?

1 ___
2 ___

3 ___
4 ___
5 ___

B
TRACK 8

Listen to the interview and match each person with the correct cell phone description.

6 ___
7 ___
8 ___
9 ___
10 ___

6 high school boy	**a** silver, thick
7 child	**b** pink with e-mail
8 businessman	**c** big, colorful
9 old man	**d** pink, without e-mail
10 high school girl	**e** black, with a small memory
	f silver, thin
	g black, with a large memory
	h shiny stickers
	i big, gray
	j black stickers

A Listen. Choose the best answers.

Total ____

A: Can I turn on the radio?

B: Go ahead, but find music that's good for studying.

A: How about **a** classical $_1$ **b** jazz?   **1** ___

B: You like that genre?

A: When I feel nervous before a test, it **a** relaxes $_2$ **b** calms me.   **2** ___

B: I think that will make me **a** sad $_3$ **b** sleepy.   **3** ___

A: Well, I don't think rock will help us.

B: **a** Neither do I $_4$ **b** I do.   **4** ___

A: So what do you want to listen to then?

B: How about reggae?

B Listen and answer the questions. (Each question is two points.)

5 When does she like to listen to music the most?   **5** ___

   a during school   **c** in the morning

   b after school   **d** at night

6 What music does he like the most?   **6** ___

   a jazz   **c** rock

   b classical   **d** pop

7 What does music give him?   **7** ___

   a a good idea   **c** some energy

   b a calm feeling   **d** a safe feeling

Self-Study

Total _____

 A

TRACK 11

Listen. Complete the sentences using the words in the box.

> **a** flying   **b** unbelievable   **c** racing   **d** weeks
>
> **e** months   **f** role-playing   **g** Wow

1 ___

A: Is that your new **1** _____ game?

B: Yeah, I finally got it.

A: How long did it take you to get it?

2 ___

B: I had to wait about two **2** _____! It was sold out everywhere.

3 ___

A: **3** _____! Have you tried it yet?

B: Yes! I've been playing all morning at home.

A: Wow. You'll be a pro soon.

4 ___

B: After I get good at this game, I'd like to try **4** _____ next.

 B

TRACK 12

Listen. Answer the three questions about the speech. (Each question is two points.)

5 ___

5 What's one reason small video game players are popular?

  a They're cheap.   **c** They're careful.

  b They're old.   **d** They're lightweight.

6 ___

6 Who uses these small video game players?

  a young people   **c** young and old people

  b old people   **d** young boys

7 ___

7 What do they have to be careful about?

  a being unpopular   **c** their money

  b their health   **d** getting older

 A   Listen. Choose the correct answer.

Total ___

Mother: **a** How ₁ **b** Where are you spending time after school these days?
I know you go somewhere.

1 ___

Boy: Oh, I stop at a coffee shop.

Mother: I didn't know you **a** like ₂ **b** drink coffee.

2 ___

Boy: Well, not so much, but I like to meet new people there.

Mother: Oh! Have you ever **a** spoken ₃ **b** talked to someone you don't know there?

3 ___

Boy: Yeah. It's really interesting to meet **a** girls ₄ **b** strangers.

4 ___

Mother: What do you talk about?

Boy: Lots of stuff. The weather, **a** music ₅ **b** sports, what's on TV . . .

5 ___

Mother: That sounds fun. Have you ever met any nice girls there?

Boy: Um, did you **a** watch ₆ **b** see that movie yesterday? How was it?

6 ___

Mother: Hey, don't try to change the topic. I asked about girls!

 B   Listen. Choose the correct answer.

7 What topic does he open the conversation with?

7 ___

  a Siberia   **c** weather

  b travel   **d** her hat

8 Which statement is correct?

8 ___

  a Both girls are shy.   **c** Both girls think the guy is cute.

  b Both girls never talk to strangers.   **d** Both girls want to meet the guy.

9 What is the new coach like?

9 ___

  a He is strict.   **c** He is tough.

  b He is friendly.   **d** We do not know.

10 What topic are they talking about today?

10 ___

  a religion   **c** music

  b England   **d** movies

Self-Study

Total _____

1 ___

2 ___

3 ___

4 ___

5 ___

6 ___

7 ___

A Listen. Choose the correct answer.

TRACK 15

A: Everyone at school knows that guy. Why is he so **a** confident ₁ **b** popular?

B: He's kind of a hero at our school.

A: A hero? Why?

B: Well, he's a strong leader and his grades are great, too.

A: I respect people who are **a** intelligent ₂ **b** brave.

B: Me, too. Do you think I can be a school hero one day?

A: That's a good question. Well, you're really **a** honest ₃ **b** polite.

B: Thanks.

A: That's an **a** interesting ₄ **b** important quality to have.

B Listen. Choose the best reply. (Each question is two points.)

TRACK 16

5 **a** Because then I can be intelligent.   **c** I don't like polite people.

   b It's not an important quality to have.   **d** Because I admire people who are polite.

6 **a** That's a terrible question.   **c** That's a tough question.

   b That's a good point.   **d** That's too hard.

7 **a** Because he's not so great.   **c** Because everyone respects him.

   b Because he is your brother.   **d** Because he is lucky.

Self-Study

A Listen. Complete the sentences using the words in the box.

TRACK 17

Total ____

a nervous	**b** strict	**c** history	**d** funny	**e** serious	**f** totally	**g** science

A: Have you seen the new **1** _____ teacher?

B: Not yet. I heard he makes students a little bit scared. What's he like?

A: Well, he looks really tough.

B: What do you mean by "tough"?

A: He has a somewhat **2** _____ face. He never smiles.

B: Is he **3** _____?

A: Well, I thought so at first. He made me **4** _____.

B: I can understand that.

A: But actually he's **5** _____.

B: Really? That's great!

1 ___

2 ___

3 ___
4 ___

5 ___

B Listen. Choose the correct answer.

TRACK 18

6 What is Mr. Tinker like today?
   a funny   **c** nice
   b strict   **d** quiet

6 ___

7 What does she mean by "enthusiastic"?
   a encouraging   **c** boring
   b talkative   **d** strict

7 ___

8 What does she think about her father?
   a He's a little bit interesting.   **c** He's totally interesting.
   b He's somewhat interesting.   **d** He's not at all interesting

8 ___

9 What kind of teacher do these students want?
   a strict   **c** kind
   b sleepy   **d** quiet

9 ___

10 What are they probably going to do next?
   a Turn right.   **c** Turn at the light.
   b Turn on the light.   **d** Study in the dark.

10 ___

Self-Study

Total _____

 A Listen. Complete the sentences using the words in the box.

TRACK 19

a spend	**b** nine	**c** five	**d** make
e great	**f** hard	**g** awful	**h** easy

A: Are you good at making money, spending money, or saving money?

1 __

B: It's **1** _____ for me to save. I'm probably best at making money.

2 __

A: That's **2** _____!

3 __

B: Well, I wish I didn't **3** _____ it so quickly. It's fun for me to shop.

A: What do you buy with it?

B: I love shopping for clothes, magazines, and music.

A: You have a part-time job, don't you?

4 __

B: Yes, I baby-sit. But I only get paid **4** _____ dollars per hour.

5 __

A: That's **5** _____!

B: I know.

 B Listen. Who spends money on what?

TRACK 20

6 __   **6** high school boy   **a** sweets

7 __   **7** high school girl   **b** shoes

8 __   **8** college student   **c** books

9 __   **9** tall girl   **d** train ticket

10 __   **10** dog walker   **e** CDs

        f motorcycle

Self-Study

 A   Listen. Choose the correct answer.

A: Have you been to the new shopping mall that just opened last month?

B: Not yet. I saw a **a** TV ₁ **b** billboard ad for it last week.

A: I saw a lot of ads on the train. I really want to go!

B: You like shopping? Perhaps we can go together then.

A: OK! Could you give me a ride in your car?

B: **a** Sure ₂ **b** No problem.

A: I can't wait. The advertising has been so **a** entertaining ₃ **b** persuasive.

B: I know!

A: I **a** guess ₄ **b** think it's had a strong effect on us!

B: Ha! You're right.

 B   Listen. Choose the correct answer. (Each question is two points.)

5 Which does the speaker NOT use to describe the Internet?

  a persuasive   **c** entertaining

  b informative   **d** careful

6 What items are on sale at the shop?

  a desk, bed, couch   **c** bed, couch, TV

  b bed, TV, couch   **d** table, desk, chair

7 What product is the commercial selling?

  a ice cream   **c** hiking shoes

  b water   **d** None of the above.

Total ____

1 ___

2 ___

3 ___

4 ___

5 ___

6 ___

7 ___

Self-Study

Total _____

A

TRACK 23

Listen. Complete the sentences using the words in the box. Two words are not use

a happy	**b** actually	**c** so	**d** fun
e really	**f** well	**g** smiling	**h** food

1 ___
2 ___
3 ___
4 ___
5 ___

6 ___

A: Wow, who are these people in this picture? They look **1** _____ excited.

B: **2** _____, that's me with my old high school friends in Las Vegas last yea

A: You all look so **3** _____. Did you win a lot of money or something?

B: No! **4** _____, we lost money.

A: Did you say you lost money? But you were **5** _____.

B: Well, we were all together again. Like old times. We just had so much

6 _____!

B

TRACK 24

Listen. Answer the questions about the talk. (Each question is two points.)

7 ___

7 How many types of people does the speaker talk about?

a one   **c** three

b two   **d** four

8 ___

8 Which type does the speaker think the world needs?

a The type that has goals.   **c** Neither type.

b The type that doesn't want to change.   **d** Both types.